**CCSS** Genre Expository T

 Essential Question
How do teams work together?

Firefighting Heroes

by Kate Sinclair

Introduction

Long ago, people used fire to live. They used it to cook and keep warm. But **accidental** fires were dangerous.

Early settlers usually made their homes from wood. There was no running water to put out fires. There were no fire departments. A fire could quickly **destroy** a town or city!

The Great Fire of London destroyed thousands of homes.

In 1666, there was a big fire in London, England. The fire burned for three days. Many houses burned down. Many people died.

The fire started as a small fire in a shop. It was a windy day. The wind moved the fire quickly across the city.

People knew they had to work together to protect themselves.

STOP AND CHECK

Why did the big fire in London spread so quickly?

CHAPTER 1
United We Stand

Fire was a problem for the first settlers in America. In 1608, a fire raced through Jamestown in Virginia. It destroyed most houses in the **colony**. There were also two **harmful** fires in Boston in 1653 and 1676.

The settlers knew that they had to **respond** quickly to fires. They formed firefighting teams of **volunteers**. Their **purpose** was to prevent and fight fires.

In the 1600s, buckets of water were kept outside each house at night. If there was a fire, volunteers used long poles to collect the buckets. Then they raced to the fire with the water.

Fire harmed many buildings in American cities.

William Penn started the city of Philadelphia in 1682. He tried to prevent fire when he planned the city. People had to clean their chimneys often. Many buildings were built from brick, not wood.

This is the first fire engine built in the United States.

Ben Franklin was one of the people who helped start America. He set up a volunteer firefighting group in Philadelphia.

Franklin started a fire brigade called The Union Fire Company. It had 30 volunteers. These volunteers were **heroes** in their community.

Ben Franklin set up a firefighting team in Philadelphia in 1736.

The first woman volunteer firefighter was Molly Williams. She was an African American. She fought fires wearing a dress and an apron. Marina Betts was another volunteer. She threw water at men who wouldn't help fight fires!

Working together was important for the volunteer firefighters. The volunteers made a line. They passed buckets of water from one person to another. They could reach the fire more quickly.

Firefighters use modern **equipment** today. **Fewer** volunteers are needed. But the job of a volunteer firefighter is just as important. Firefighters still need to work as a team.

STOP AND CHECK

How did William Penn and Ben Franklin help fight fires?

Firefighters put out a fire in Atlanta, Georgia.

CHAPTER 2

Firefighters at Work

Today, there are thousands of fire departments across the United States. More than 800,000 volunteers help run them. Volunteers have a sense of **civic duty**. They want to help their community.

Today, firefighters use modern equipment, such as high-pressure hoses, to fight fires.

Firefighters work with other teams, such as paramedics.

Firefighters work in teams. Firefighters learn different jobs. They learn to drive the fire truck. They learn to set up the hoses and ladders. They learn to go into a burning building safely.

Volunteer firefighters do other work, too. They help during natural **disasters**, car accidents, and medical emergencies.

Volunteer firefighters need **training**. They learn about fire safety. They have to pass a **physical** test. Firefighters have to crawl on their hands and knees through small spaces. They have to move ladders. They have to drag heavy hoses and carry them on stairs. They also must be able to carry an adult through a doorway.

Firefighters wear protective gear. They carry heavy equipment.

Radius/SuperStock

All in a Day's Work

Read about this firefighter's day.

The alarm is ringing. A house is on fire. We run to the fire truck. When we get to the fire, it is hard to control. We wear protective gear and breathing equipment. My job is to control the hose. Anne takes care of the ladders. We get everyone out of the house. A man is finding it hard to breathe. Peter, our first aid officer, takes care of him. Our new equipment helps make sure the fire is out. We are all tired, but everyone is safe.

Firefighters work together at a fire.

STOP AND CHECK

What things do volunteer firefighters need to be able to do?

CHAPTER 3
Safety in the Home

Firefighters teach people about fire **prevention** and fire safety. Do you know what to do if there is a fire at your home?

Escape!

Talk to your family about the best ways to get out of the house. Choose a place away from the house to meet. Choose someone to count people to make sure everyone is out of the house. Call the fire department as soon as you can. Go outside first.

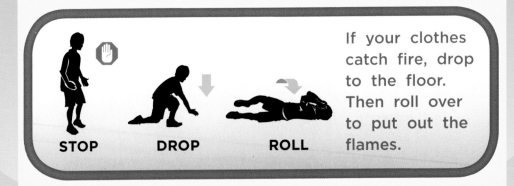

STOP   **DROP**   **ROLL**

If your clothes catch fire, drop to the floor. Then roll over to put out the flames.

High-Rise Buildings

Make sure you know where each **exit** is if you live in a tall building. When you get outside, stay out. Tell the fire department if you think anyone is still inside.

Stairs are the safest way out of a tall building during a fire.

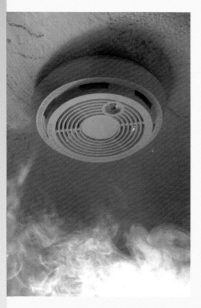

A working smoke alarm saves lives!

Smoke Alarms

A working smoke alarm can tell you there is a fire. Make sure your home has smoke alarms. Change the batteries every six months.

STOP AND CHECK

What are some things to remember if there is a fire in your home?

Conclusion

People have known for a long time that **teamwork** helps protect the community from fires. Today many people have busy lives. It can be hard to find time to volunteer for services such as firefighting. Even so, the work of volunteer firefighters is still very important.

Firefighters teach people about fire safety.

Respond to Reading

Summarize

Summarize the most
important information
in *Firefighting Heroes.*
Use details from the text.
Your chart may help you.

Details

↓

Point of View

Text Evidence

1. Reread Chapter 2. How does the author
   describe volunteer firefighters? Use an
   example from the text in your answer.
   AUTHOR'S POINT OF VIEW

2. Find the word *crawl* on page 10. What
   does it mean? What clues help you figure
   it out? **VOCABULARY**

3. Write a paragraph describing what the
   author thinks about volunteer firefighters.
   WRITE ABOUT READING

Compare Texts
Read about a woman who gets some unusual help.

A FAVOR REPAID

Sal Fink was the daughter of a famous Mississippi boatman. She was brave and loud.

One day, Sal saw three bear cubs sleeping in the woods. Sal bent down to pat them. Patting bears isn't a good idea, but Sal was **careless** about her safety.

Sal heard a loud growl behind her. She turned around and saw an angry mother bear. The bear was about to attack! Sal didn't move away. She yelled and then wrestled the bear to the ground. She patted the bear and walked away.

Two years later, Sal was in the forest. She was chopping down a tree. Suddenly she smelled smoke. She looked around and saw flames everywhere.

Sal didn't know which way to go. She yelled loudly, but no one heard her, or so she thought!

Suddenly a bear came running out of the trees. The bear had recognized Sal's voice. The bear was afraid of fire, but it remembered that Sal had let it live. The bear ran toward Sal. Then it ran back the way it had come. The bear wanted Sal to follow her.

Sal followed the bear, and soon they came to a river. The bear jumped in, and Sal jumped in, too. Sal grabbed the bear's fur, and it swam to the other side of the river. Sal was safe. The bear walked off into the trees, and Sal never saw it again.

Make Connections

How did Sal and the bear work together in *A Favor Repaid*? ESSENTIAL QUESTION

How do *Firefighting Heroes* and *A Favor Repaid* show teamwork? TEXT TO TEXT

Glossary

civic duty *(SIV-ik DEW-tee)* the responsibilities of a citizen *(page 8)*

colony *(KOL-uh-nee)* a place where people first live in a land that is new to them *(page 4)*

volunteers *(vol-uhn-TEERS)* people who do a job for no pay *(page 4)*

Index

Focus on Social Studies

Purpose To find out about volunteers

What to Do

Step 1 Choose a group that uses volunteers, such as a food bank or an animal shelter.

Step 2 Find out all you can about the group. Find out how the group works. Find out its goal.

Step 3 Find out what volunteers do.

Step 4 Write a short paragraph about what the group does.

Step 5 Write a short paragraph about what volunteers do.

Conclusion What did you learn about the organization?